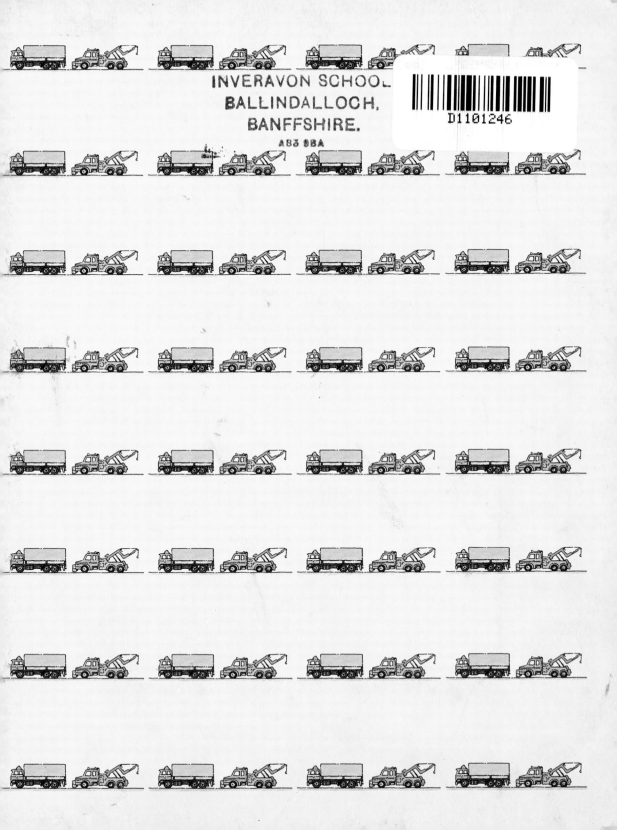

A DORLING KINDERSLEY BOOK

Senior Editor Jane Yorke
Editor Dawn Sirett
Senior Art Editor Mark Richards
Art Editor Jane Coney
Production Marguerite Fenn

Photography by Stephen Oliver
Illustrations by Jane Cradock-Watson
and Dave Hopkins
**Truck consultant and models
supplied by** Ted Taylor

Eye Openers ®

First published in Great Britain in 1991
by Dorling Kindersley Limited,
9 Henrietta Street, London WC2E 8PS
Reprinted 1991

Copyright © 1991
Dorling Kindersley Limited, London

A CIP catalogue record for this book is
available from the British Library.

ISBN 0-86318-458-8

Reproduced by Colourscan, Singapore
Printed and bound in Italy by L.E.G.O., Vicenza

·EYE·OPENERS·

Trucks

DORLING KINDERSLEY
London • New York • Stuttgart

Delivery truck

Delivery trucks make short trips. They deliver goods to shops. The back of the truck rolls up for easy unloading.

cab

TURBO INTERCOOLING 2800

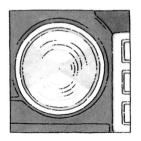 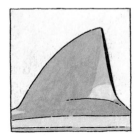

light air deflector

Snow plough

In winter, a snow plough is used to clear snow from the roads. The large plough blade pushes the snow into big piles. The dumper at the back carries grit. The back tips up and scatters grit on to the icy road.

plough blade

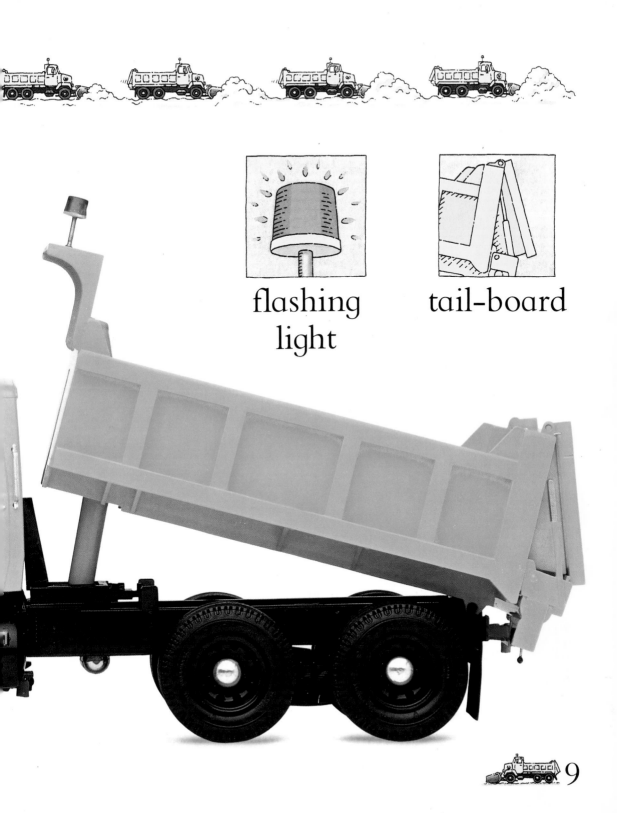

flashing
light

tail-board

9

Concrete mixer

This truck delivers concrete to building sites. The concrete is made in the big mixing drum. The drum turns round and round. The concrete pours out down the chute at the back.

bonnet

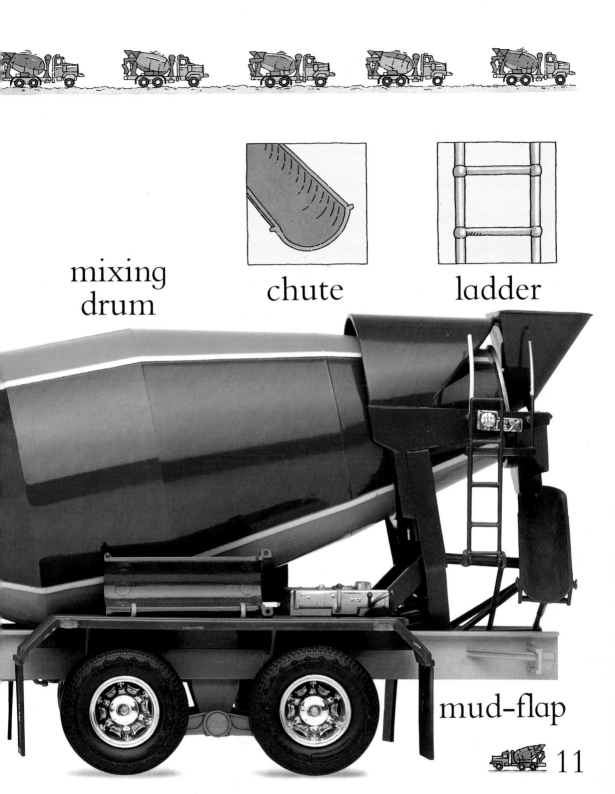

mixing
drum

chute

ladder

mud-flap

11

Fire engine

A fire engine has a long ladder. It reaches to the top of tall buildings. The fireman climbs up the ladder and stands in the cage. He rescues people from smoke and flames.

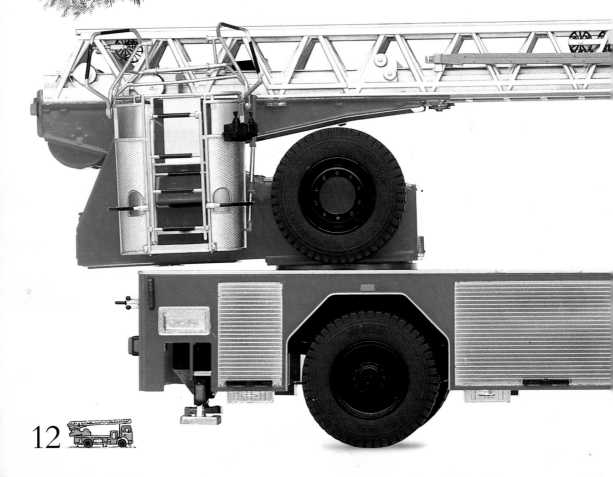

flashing light

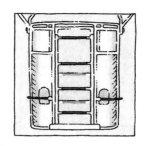
cage

water hose

ladder

SDF 304

F613

Crane truck

This truck has a crane to lift heavy loads like concrete slabs or bricks. It can unload materials at building sites quickly and easily. The legs at the back hold the truck steady.

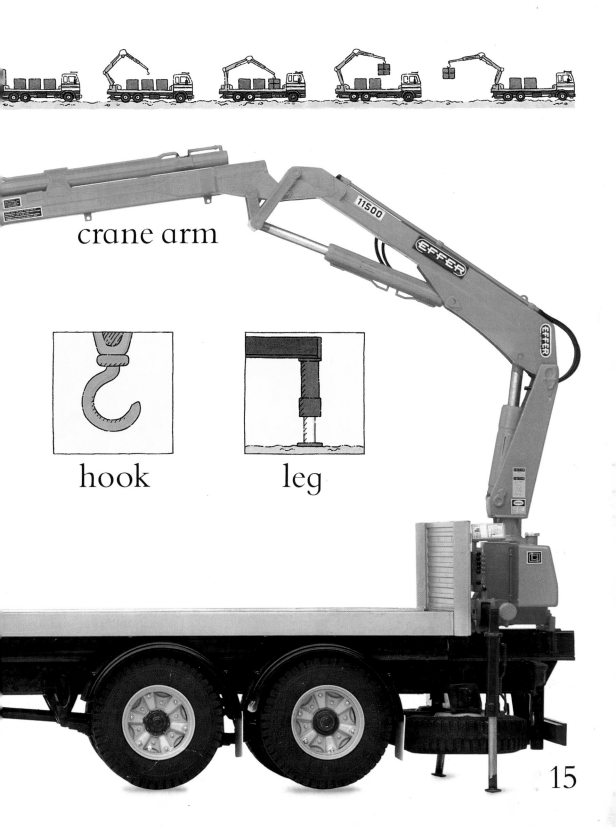

crane arm

hook

leg

15

Tanker

Trucks called tankers are used to transport petrol. Petrol is carried in the big tank at the back. At the petrol station the petrol is pumped down a hose into underground tanks.

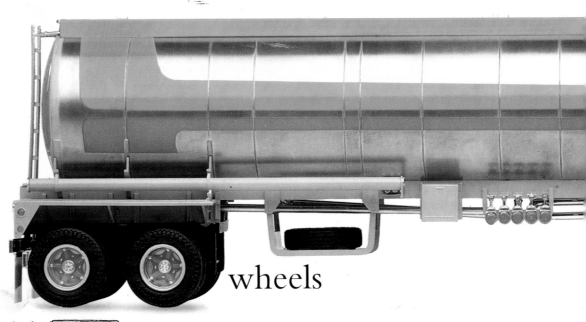

wheels

hose

rear-view
mirror

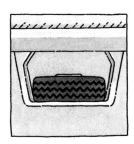

spare
wheel

tank

air
deflector

Tow truck

A tow truck rescues cars that have broken down or had an accident. The car is hooked on to the crane at the back. The truck tows the car to a garage for repairs.

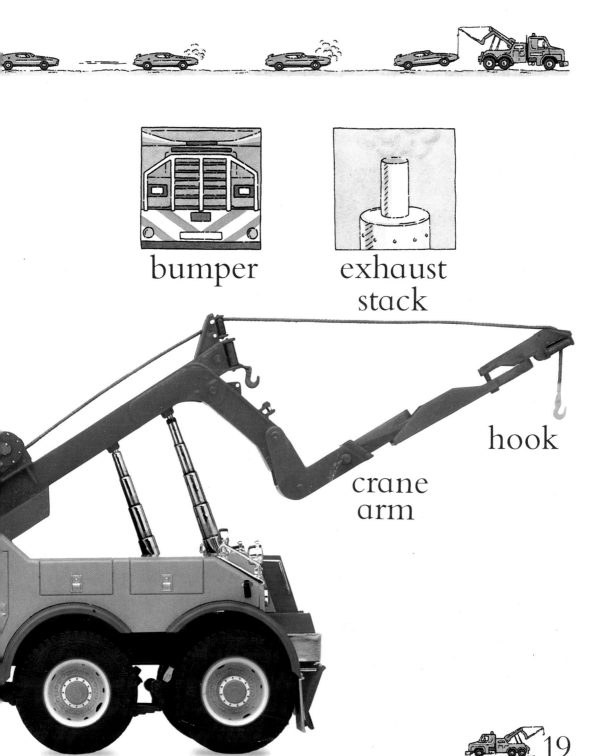

bumper

exhaust
stack

hook

crane
arm

19

Car transporter

Car transporters can carry lots of cars at once. The cars can be driven on and off using the ramp. The cab of this truck tips forward, so that the mechanic can work on the engine.

tipper
cab

engine

ramp

trailer